THE Donkey Elegies

AN ESSAY IN POEMS

The Donkey Elegies: An Essay in Poems
Copyright © 2020 by Nickole Brown

Cover art by Tiffany Bozic: *Donkey*, 2020

Cover design by Seth Pennington

Author photograph by Joli Livaudais

The epigraph is an excerpt from the poem "Beauty and the Beast" by Eleanor Wilner, first published in *Sarah's Choice* (University of Chicago Press, 1990) and later in *Reversing the Spell: New & Selected Poems* (Copper Canyon Press, 1997).

Sibling Rivalry Press, LLC
PO Box 26147
Little Rock, AR 72221

info@siblingrivalrypress.com

www.siblingrivalrypress.com

ISBN: 978-1-943977-71-0

By special invitation, this title is housed in the Rare Book and Special Collections Vault of the Library of Congress.

First Sibling Rivalry Press Edition, January 2020

THE Donkey Elegies

AN ESSAY IN POEMS

NICKOLE BROWN

SIBLING RIVALRY PRESS
DISTURB/ENRAPTURE
LITTLE ROCK, ARKANSAS

THE DONKEY Elegies

AN ESSAY IN POEMS

NICKOLE BROWN

SIBLING RIVALRY PRESS

"We, who burned our brand
into the uncomplaining flank
of creation, begin to hope
for what may yet survive us . . .
and as the animals grow
smaller, moving off into a blue, inhuman
distance, we dare not call out
after them: 'Good luck!'
for fear our best-meant words, straight
from the heart, will follow them
as they depart, and curse them."

—Eleanor Wilner

1.

Ears like sugar scoops. Ears like hands cupped to cradle a cool drink from the creek. Ears like single petals of dahlias—at full bloom, curled, firmly upright but always soft, always open.

Furred periscopes, one pivots to the wheezing scream of a squirrel above,

and I follow, hear as if for the first time that common arboreal cry neither chirp nor growl but something in between, like the caw of a mother blue jay stoked behind the teeth of an old yard dog.

Your other ear—blessed as I am—rotates towards me.

Sweet apricots, velvet
satellites, the twin souls
atop the head of every donkey.

2.

I am no cowgirl, no farrier, no vet, but still I learn the routine: how to fit the halter around your face, how to sweetsong you back to the barn, insistent as you rightly are we stop to pay homage to the wet green of new grass.

With a brush I shoofly your twitching withers, scrub the mud from your hindquarters to mink your coat up again, then bend on knee as if to propose, lifting your fetlock to face the bottom of your foot to me.

There I scour the tender dark with a metal pick, try to ease the place where your sole argues with the bone that nestles it, dislodging sand and shit and tiny stones—careful, so careful, afraid as I am of a swift kick that could break my neck, worried as I am about the many ailments that could sour your gait if I get this wrong: seedy toe and white line disease, abscess, laminitis, thrush brought on from too much North Carolina rain.

I memorize the names as I touch them, whispering,

heel, hoof wall, sole, toe, frog—breathe the cave-cricketing dank that hides there, that baked-bread fecundity, a scent not unlike the sweet decay of a barn, a rank comfort under that stoic surefootedness for which you're known, the who-would-have-known vulnerability secreted under the steps of every donkey.

3.

At this animal park, I work to be near

your otherworldly greeting, a thing you show off again and again, hollering
while you inhale and hollering while you exhale, hollering while you breath
in *and* out, a didgeridoo kind of circular yowling, a way to play no other
mammal can manage, a pleading that peals a juke band of *hurrays* anytime I
bring fresh hay. But no one hears

what I hear. Instead, passersby can't help but laugh and laugh. To them, the
hollering smacks of stupidity, or maybe orgasm, the open-window kind heard
from the street, urgent and hotly

embarrassing. They offer crude imitations, guffaw their Old MacDonald versions
of your song, their fake brays of *Eeyore, Hee Haw, Eeyore, Hee Haw* as they pass
us by.

Onomatopoetic maybe, but wrong. The real sound

is the world's largest door swung wide, an open throat of rust and hinge, the
caustic rocketing of a mother goose if she were born horse, a trumpeting
animated by Dr. Seuss. This call is meant to travel, and far—miles and miles
across a vast expanse of desert—made to survive the dry lonely for which this
animal was made.

I lean into the gyrating see-saws of tone, try to understand the shameless,
insistent language of donkeys.

4.

Eeyore, once an early Egyptian word for an animal believed sacred, now the name of the stitched-back-together low note of Prozac feeding on thistles in Pooh's Hundred Acre Wood. For his birthday, an empty honey jar and a popped red balloon; for his detachable tail, a pink bow Owl mistakes for a bell pull.

Disney, famous for jump-starting the heart of a child's worst fear—always wiping out the beloved mother in the first scene—Walt, sly manipulator, pins the tail back on the stuffed beast with a black tack.

Goodnight nobody,

one bedtime story read. Funny, how early in life sorrow came to me as a kind of comfort—hardly did I feel sorry for you then,

dear melancholy donkey.

5.

Scroll down the screen. Click on

a billy goat prancing on the back of a jenny, click on a black cat snoozing on the back of a jack, on other donkeys rolling in the snow, jockeying a beach ball, playing tug-of-war with a fire hose, scaring a prissy peacock out of the yard. Click on

a baby donkey sleep-twitching in a hammock, a baby donkey dream-kicking in a girl's arms, the scene so bucolic you know it's staged. Click on

a donkey braying at a digital screen displaying his own picture, braying for banana peels, braying along to a song fiddled in his barn. Click

and watch a donkey monkey the latch with her lips to sneak herself and four others out of their corral. This is my kind of porn—the kind I need when I've clicked on

coral wasting disease bleaching the sea floor, on penguins washing up on tropical beaches and dolphins washing up into the jaws of a polar bear, all our currents gone wrong, wrong, wrong while the military shrugs and drops the mother of all bombs.

The first time I actually saw a donkey, I was traipsing abroad, trying out my poor Spanish in Mexico. Who knows if Pedro was really his name, but that's what us tourists were told, and his trick was to lip up a bottle and throw his head back to gulp beer, fraternity-style. There was no internet then, certainly no phones to bear witness or look up roadside party tricks like this to figure if what I saw was right or wrong.

Did I laugh? Or did I actually see that emaciated swayback crusted with fleas and guzzling beer, a chorus of skeletal dogs exhausted in the dirt road? I cannot say. Worse, I think maybe I thought

very little at all, and like most of us, I bought a Coke and got back on the bus.

Twenty years later, and here is this feed of little clips streaming by, each one making me look back and realize there was a living being worth saving, an animal I once didn't see at all.

6.

Fur the color of fawn grass—long, bending, done in by the sun—or else fur the carbonated gray of fog so thick it looks like the mountains here, on fire with dawn.

Down your neck and from shoulder to shoulder, two dark lines make an X, marks the spot, and some call those ridges *eel stripes* and others say the capital-*f* father himself drew that crucifix across your back.

But I'm not fooled into thinking your liquid blinking and Maybelline lashes make a gentle beast:

like my mama and hers before, donkeys do not scare but stand their ground, don't take off running as those gorgeous, high-class horses do. In danger, a herd will face inward to huddle around its foals, tightening a circle of *go ahead and try me,* daring any predator near their fatal chorus line of kicking legs.

Yes, any farmer knows you're a more savage guardian than any dog, and I recognize you as one of my own. Fierce matriarch, you'll stomp a hawk near your flock of hens, chase a bear away from your bleating sheep, smash the white brains from a coyote who tries its teeth on a weaker donkey.

7.

Don't confuse the two: a donkey is not exactly mule—

the first belongs to itself, all raw chromosomes in place,

the other is government-issued, manufactured by a jack rearing up higher than
he should to drill into a horse harnessed tight and held still by a farmer who
longs for her strong and sterile foal. Can you hear

what's been made by that one syllable—*mule*—more prod than word, an easy
whip-crack yelled over and over to drive a beast, to make him work?

Mule, mule, mule.
Gitalong, mule. Giddyup, mule, giddyap.
This is donkey made

stronger plow, made into something kin to beer—pure *draught*, or put the
American way, made *draft*, made compulsory, forced into conscription, like
all those boys in my mama's class that won that twisted lottery and came home
from Vietnam unable to tell the slam of a screen door from a land mine.

So let us call a mule for what he is—a coal-mine donkey, an asbestos-mine
donkey, a down-dark-into-the-trenches-and-bombs donkey, an engine, a device,
a tool, a young thing that didn't know better than to do what he was told.

8.

On your back:
Greeks, Italians, Ethiopians, Arabs, Appalachians.

On your back:
drunk cowboys, drunk tourists, birthday girls in powder blue, this season's dead deer, this season's dead turkeys, a wolf shot dead in her tracks, boys playing cowboy who sling pellet guns and pretend dead.

On your back:
roped-together televisions, computers, pallets of bricks, bushels of firewood, sloshing tanks of well water and sloshing kegs of brew, boxes of bullets, sow-sized bags of rice heavy

as a setting sun, or as they say in Istanbul, *heavy as a donkey that's dead.*

The corners of your mouth froth, rip at the bit. Your joints grind down to bone on bone. Finally, your back, it sways, it bends in the middle as does a shelf that's been asked to hold more than it possibly can, before it eventually splits,

exposing spine. Overloaded, the cart
tips back, suspends in the air
the limp donkey.

9.

On your back:
Christ, five days before,

into Jerusalem, on a colt found tied to a door, a juvenile commandeered for the parade—only a foal, really, a donkey so new he'd never been ridden, a wobbly thing on knock knees, covered in apostles' cloaks and led through a hosanna crowd that will, in a few days, call for the execution of what they now praise.

What being better fit for the job, to burden this passive, locust-eating man on the way to

his slaughter? They say even stones sang out, that sucklings gave their milk-tongues in praise. A confetti of blossoms and grain. A road littered with palm fronds and olive branches, willow and yew. A crush of fans frantic to be saved. Do you see the

whites of that wild-eyed animal, the sclera lit by such fervor? Do you see how he pains to move through the mob, how easy for those young legs to buckle and slip, how precarious the procession of any chosen donkey?

10.

On your back:
soldiers, soldiers, more soldiers.

On your back:
the weight of Victory scraps, kitbags of mess tins and bayonets, canteens and binoculars, cases of Lucky Strikes, cans of fish flesh and cans of cow flesh, cans of unidentified flesh gelatinized and named SPAM.

In the first war, you carry picks and shovels used to gash open the earth, you carry the rag scraps of bodies from the fields up to the operating table then quietly back out of the tent.

In those trenches are 80,000 other donkeys and mules recruited alongside horses and dogs and camels, fitted with gas masks for photos in that funny-not-funny kind of souvenir trauma makes, just desperate to have a good time. In that ravaged

sky, a whole metropolis of pigeons frenzy their way to what they think is home, tattered little notes rolled and slid into a tube clamped to their legs.

All night in the foxholes,
the terrified boys bury their faces in your warm neck, soft-talk to you of home, but you are silent—for battle, all vocal cords are cut within the throats of donkeys.

11.

The second time
the world goes to war, donkeys are airlifted, shoved out hatches with parachutes
strapped to their backs. A whimsical sight,

maybe—

all those Balthazars aloft—until the panicked beasts brace for landing

and shatter a drove of knees.

Those that hit the ground alive almost look peaceful if you don't know better:

how quiet they are, how still they lay their weary form over the crumpled
origami of their legs. Bewildered and in shock, they look around as quiet as
the tethered silk billows down like a shroud. In their expression a stunned
blankness that barely has a chance to ask why

before they are answered

with one clean shot between the eyes.

Breach, cleft, compound, hemorrhage, fracture—the foot soldier knows the
killing is the worst kind of mercy, but still, he can't help but look up and
chuckle: in the air, still alive,

another flying donkey.

12.

Who can say if Adam understood the consequences of his task, but each word
we give to name an animal is a sentence, a decision made by the court tribunal
that is us:

the difference between *dog* and *cur*, *cow* and *stock*, between *deer* and *game*,
possum and *vermin*, *mouse* and *feeder* is

the difference between a wheel to run on versus a glue trap, a copper cowbell
or a stockyard-style knocker of electricity meant to stun before the blood is
drained.

Now, call a donkey a *jackass* and you make the animal into a classic punch-

line of the kingdom, a defense against recognizing who made us, against giving
thanks to a being we once couldn't live without, the same as I was once too
good for my illiterate, hammer-swinging grandfather who taught me how to
pray. How I teased all his backwards mispronunciations, a shame that burns
within me to this day.

Worse, call a donkey *feral,* and you've cinched a Judas collar around the neck
of a jenny, duped her with a tracking device that leads a helicopter of marksmen
who take out one wild herd then the next and the next as she keeps searching
out a family before she's the last

to be shot.

Before, in war, she and her kind were necessary, allies capable of going where
none other could, scrambling up uneven ground, surviving on the hot nothing
of dry scrub and air, named

Sergeant Biscuits, Major Hazel, Pete the Trigger, Jane the Brave.

But after the treaties are signed, they're an invasive diaspora, a destroyer of
cultivated fields, an unowned pest, good for the bone meal in dog food. And
always, the bounty is paid on the ears of each dead donkey.

13.

In the Kentucky that made me, long before I was born, coal was the darkness
torn from the dark, and donkeys the color of cave fish and moonlight hauled
the ore cars, a history told by a few black-and-white photos and those few men
not yet dead from black lung. It meant nothing

to me—not the black coal or the white donkeys—not those worked-to-the-
bone workers nor the glow of their tractable brutes, those donkeys ghosted
deep underground so long they would emerge decades later

completely blind. Angry and young, I was ready to kill off any part of me that
smacked of those hillbilly roots, and in a basement reeking of cat piss and
strawberry wine, we did our best to blow apart

speakers with heavy metal cranked loud. We let a blindfold do its work before
spinning ourselves round and round, swinging a bat until one of us hit what we
were aiming for with a satisfactory thud, thrilled to hear all those plastic-wrapped
hard candies hit the concrete floor. Little did we know we were acting out

our own trashy sort of morality play, what was really spilling from the split
side of that white piñata, from that cheap paper mache donkey.

14.

The truth of my family was buried in their talk:

the church ladies would say they hadn't seen me *in a donkey's years* even if I had
missed only a few Sundays, and all us kids knew to avoid Uncle Leon because
the man *could talk the hind legs off a donkey* and that telling grandfather what
to do *was about as good as putting a steering wheel on a mule.*

By then, not one of us kept animals anymore. No, we were ready to let the city
and its money make us clean and new, opened our homes to nothing more
than a teacup poodle with toenails painted pink. But still, our etymologies
remembered

what we'd rather forget, because if we had something to carry anything before,
it was surely nothing more than a good-for-nothing donkey, because rarely did
our beasts of burden include a horse unless—you know how the saying goes—
we were *hungry enough to eat one.*

But here
in this field sweetened with the low mumbling of grouse and a wind that flips
maple leaves silver, this donkey is perfectly still as if he's always been here and
never left, as if he's always been this way and always will. And who would
dream of letting him go? When I dirty my nails scratching his stout neck, it's
like touching the source of all those country sayings that formed my tongue
as a child, as if each syllable were a hayseed that could grow into a real something
of use, as if each word was once an animal we'd left behind,

exhausted and in shame as we
were. And now, only now
can I reclaim
what I didn't even know
was missing and there
find myself.

15.

Caretaking ain't much more than scooping poop.

That's what mama said.

Shit tending. Then she laughed, recalled when I was still shitting green—*Poor baby. It was clear up your back to your neck.* Then, returning to the dishes as not to choke up, said, *I never did mind the mess my babies made.*

I won't say this is the same, but when the community-service punk clocked for speeding with a rattle of beer cans on his floorboards can't get over the fact I clean the barn for free because I *want to*, I know what my mother meant. He roughnecks the goats, grabs their horns like he might a motorcycle's handlebars, looks over at me in the donkey pen, says, *Fuckin disgusting, if you ask me.*

But maybe he's right:

only minutes and the new pile clogs the air with a swarm, and I can't help but notice the subtle flinch of visitors, their pity seeing a grown woman shovel shit. I imagine they sense the life I was born into, the one I was meant to have, not much different from any other up or down my matrilineal line, a birthright that would've never let me see a day in school past tenth grade, and by the time I'd even think about going back for my diploma, I'd be trapped with too many babies and a shit husband to boot. But what they couldn't imagine is though I escaped all that, all those years behind the desk have unstitched me from my body in another way, how this grunt work is my repair of the soul.

I lug what I'm able to the compost. The heavy bucket squeaks, something in its bent handle a seagull begging bread, and happy for once, I make a kind of song in my fool head. I scoop and haul, scoop and haul, scoop and haul, say a giggly-lady ditty to myself, lullaby it the way I might to a colicky baby, soothing,

sweet donkey, hungry gull, sweet gull, hungry donkey, hungry gull, sweet donkey.

16.

Mary knew.

Tupped by the almighty, she was no fool now, knew that bright singe was the small, dark crown of a half-God insisting, making his way through the small door between her legs.

Slumped in the swaying saddle, broken water wetting her blue robe black, her pains divine, she clutched the dusty tufts, yanked the hair from the root, took for her suffering the steady,

uncomplaining mane of a donkey.

17.

Did I really say *I'm sorry* when the man's grocery cart steamrolled my foot, *sorry*
when the postman flung that fragile package on the stoop, *sorry* when the boss
took credit for my work then demanded another run to the copy machine?
Did I actually giggle and smile

at the player who bragged about his wife then tried to slip a roofie into my
drink? And did I apologize again as I politely made my exit, never putting my
back to him as if he were the damn Queen of England? And really, how many
people told me what a good,

good girl I was? I smiled at the man who cat-called me from the scaffolding,
smiled at the man on the subway who traced the seam of my jeans with the
tip of his index, smiled at the man who shoved my friend down the cellar stairs
and barred the door, smiled at the man who married another friend then did
unspeakable things with a fast-food worker in a parking lot. Did I smile

hard enough, smile so hard
they might not
hurt us anymore?

Fawning is one way to dodge what's coming when you've no other way to fight.

Tractable is one way a domestic avoids extinction.

It took me decades
to step into the barn and ask these questions
of a donkey who learned to survive
as I did, who placidly moved forward,
regardless, in spite of everything,
just like me.

18.

Hung like a. Bigger than a.

All the big D jokes, a drunk uncle's sick metaphor:
the best of that man's three legs just a swingin like a baby's arm holding an apple.

And no matter how you try to block it, the spam keeps coming—never once
do you click on the obscene link, but the subject line alone conjures a teenage
girl torn in half by a donkey.

At the bar, the boys yuck it up, pass the pitcher, go on and on:

Hey. Have you heard this one? A donkey walks into a bar.
   No, wait, that one's old as shit. Wait.

Hey, how do you compliment a donkey owned by a chick?
   You say, "Hey, gal, nice ass!"

Hey, what do you get when cross a donkey with a habanero?
   A piece of ass that'll bring a tear to your eye!

Or, *hey, hey, hey. Wait. This one's the best: If a chick's got a donkey and a man's got
a rooster and her donkey eats his rooster, what do you have?*

I interrupt the punch-line before they get too crass, but then they turn to me:

*Really, Nick? Really? After all those years in college, you're writing about donkeys?
You've got to be kidding me, you can't be serious . . . you're flat-out serious, aren't
you? I mean, really. A "noble beast"? Noble beast . . . my ass!*

I try to laugh or at least not be the uptight bookworm they've known all their
life. Besides, behind their jokes

is not the animal itself but the animal
they see, not the animal they know
but the animal they think.

19.

There are some jokes they won't say, at least not while I'm at the table, but I know how it goes:

The type of gal that lets men take her back door so to speak is a *donkey slut*. Then,

once she's used up for good,

once she's been *stomped hard,*

what's left of her should come

as no surprise:

that place from which all of us were pushed into this world, that place they once ached to touch, is now done for, is *rode hard and put up wet*, is a *stank pelt*, is a *stench trench*, is one *nasty, stomped donkey.*

20.

Ungulate: such a throat-stuck word, *ugly* buried right there in its syllables, just as where I'm from, *capable* is mostly a word for a woman *ugly as sin,* most likely with an ass to be worked off. Can you see me,

my once-young skin fluorescent-lit, a nametag pinned to my polyester shirt? Can you see the cashier who stood with me as I bagged, the brace she had to wear squeezing up rolls on her back when she reached to scan your chips and cans? Or do you see me, years later, asking if you want a warm-up on that coffee, if I can get you some catsup to go with that? I went to school, found a way out, but somewhere is another me studying the schedule at the bus stop, clutching her pocketbook to her lap, eyeing the steady river of traffic passing her with just one person in nearly every car. Do we dismiss sturdy, useful beings because we despise what we're afraid we'll become?

Or is it just familiarity that breeds contempt?

Foam and blood of the bit, strain of the yoke, clay so damn rain-heavy and red it's bound to snap the legs that sink too deep and still try to pull.

Don't say, *stubborn.* Don't say, *thick* or *slow* or *capable, bless her heart.*

No. Say, *thank you.* Say, *please.*

Say, *I see you.* Now, slow down. Pull over.

Look out over that fence and tell me if through the rain you don't recognize,

standing there,
that beautiful, necessary,
weary donkey.

21.

Pule: a word for milk made much like ours, closer to that of the human breast than any other mammal's.

Light and sweet, a keeper of beauty, the secret ingredient warmed into Cleopatra's baths and made into face masks of bread soaked in that frothy drink for the haughty faces of Napoleon's sister and Nero's wife.

Known as elixir for agues and blood fluxes, seen by the doctors of Paris as the best wet nurse to fatten a wan orphan back from skin and bones,

this was once the salvation of abandoned children and doorstep infants, of waifs and failures-to-thrive who had their hungry mouths brought straight to those gray teats to latch and suckle

the kindness of donkeys.

22.

Balaam, with an *a* in his name to mark each time he thrashed his donkey that day so long ago, but we all know if the counting counted the beatings of that man's whole short-tempered life, we'd call him by an endless outcry of that terrified vowel, a long, continuous howl:

Baaaaaaaaaaaaaaaaaaaaaaaaaaaaaaaaalaaaaaaaaaaaaaaaaaaaaaaaaaaaaam, with more letters than I care to write.

Beat the living shit out of her, mama would say, so I can't help but imagine hot green streaks scared down that donkey's hind legs, can't help but wince at the cracking that staff made when she turned from the path he chose, avoiding what that man could not see.

Only twice in the Bible does an animal speak, and this was no hissing mouthpiece of temptation. No, all she had were questions:

What have I done to you to make you beat me?

and

Am I not your own donkey, which you have always ridden, to this day?

So, if we believe God
reached in to miracle that donkey's throat, could it be those words were meant for us all? If so, what have any of us done to answer? And what have I to say for myself?

If I muck the barn and scatter the hay, if I sweep the steps and measure the grain, for which of my own ignorances and indifferences am I atoned when the living world was speaking to me and I did not

hear nor care to listen? There is no angel I deserve to see, but still, I'm trying to stop and step from the path when I'm told, trying to understand the voice ready to thunder-strike in a most fire-and-brimstone way, the one that said, *Yes, you I certainly would have killed. But I would have spared the donkey.*

30

23.

Hebrews were once called *donkey lovers*, an Egyptian slur meant to equate one with the other, but when the waters cracked opened and parted, still, those terrified people coaxed their terrified familiars across the sea floor to freedom. And the donkey, a book says, is the only significant domesticated species from Africa. So let's have out with it:

Two kinds of backs
broken to make civilization,
both considered animals,
one human, one not.

Put another way, who carried us from that squat existence of flint strike to entire cities lit so bright the capillaries of their fire can be seen from space?

Who blistered and tore, who blew their knees and threw out their vertebrae hauling the stones and laying the tracks, plowing one field and then the next? Who took the brunt of the two-by-four, who was branded and put to stud and became a target for rope practice, then worked some more?

We know the answer but are ashamed, too ashamed, to say. The answer is one but not and never the same. The answer is a slave.

24.

Noah knew.

Or at least those artists painting the scene did, with a donkey carrying his family into the dark of that stifling ark before the flood hit.

And here we are, on the brink again, testing the promise of rainbows with who-knows-how-many continents' worth of glacial melt and less and less forest to save. There is no beauty

in nature I see anymore
that I recognize
as simply beautiful
without adding a prayer
of *please, don't die.*

Even now, one hungry country is rounding up the last of the donkeys in another, buying them cheap to skin into medicinal gelatin and grind the rest into burger, and on those same ships

are loaded pangolin scales and rhino horn, even the last of our box turtles stolen from these very hills I now make home.

I do not mean to preach. It's so unbecoming of poetry, and no one wants to hear how much we'll need to be carried out of this

on the humble and strong
backs of donkeys,
if there are any left.

25.

Blessed be. You know how it goes:
Inherit the.

In the stall, I stop for a pleasing
sound, a steady prayer
deep in the mill of teeth.

An echo within his long and humble
skull, a plain song of persistence, of hunger
met with plenty of time to chew.

Listen.

Can you hear it too?

In his dutiful mouth, the pulp and resignation,
the grit and patience of every
thing grown by the sun surrendered
but saved, brought back

by the common, low-life, baseborn, absolute

holiness that is
this donkey.

ACKNOWLEDGMENTS

My favorite word is *sanctuary*, and my deepest gratitude goes to those who work to give that word meaning to orphaned, injured, and unwanted animals. In particular, this includes those in my hometown who welcomed me into their facilities and trusted me with their animals, including Shannon and Richard Knapp of Heart of Horse Sense, Savannah Trantham and Kimberly Brewster of Appalachian Wild, and Trina Hudson and Barbara Bellows of Animal Haven of Asheville. I especially want to lend my heartfelt gratitude to poet Jody Stewart for both her support of these poems (and time to write alongside her beloved donkey, Macaroni), as well as to the plucky and knowledgeable Ben Wilson at the Western North Carolina Nature Center and the two donkeys he allowed me to tend there.

I also want to thank my wife Jessica Jacobs, who endured nearly three years' worth of drafts as I was trying to write this sequence and was instrumental in helping me craft and articulate what I needed to say. As always, you're my best reader, and rarely do you hesitate to kiss me in greeting even when I come home covered head-to-toe in what I've mucked from the barn, and never once did you fuss when all eighty-plus of those Animal Series volumes from Reaktion Books arrived at the house, all at once. (The *Donkey* volume from that series— written by Jill Bough of Australia—informed and inspired this sequence in so many ways, and for her compassion and research I'm also thankful.)

My gratitude to the amazing Seth Pennington and Bryan Borland at Sibling Rivalry Press for their ongoing support of my work, especially for taking a look at a very early draft of these poems years ago and believing in them, even then.

In addition, I want to thank Tiffany Bozic for creating the soulful donkey that graces this cover. As always, she paints what I wish I could write.

Finally, I'd like to extend a word of acknowledgment to the Peaceful Valley Donkey Rescue in Texas and The Donkey Sanctuary in Devon, England. Both of these organizations are doing the hard work to care for these misunderstood animals and to raise awareness about their plight.

All proceeds from this book will go to the animal rehabs and sanctuaries mentioned here.

ABOUT THE AUTHOR

NICKOLE BROWN received her MFA from the Vermont College, studied literature at Oxford University, and was the editorial assistant for the late Hunter S. Thompson. She worked at Sarabande Books for ten years. Her first collection, *Sister*, a novel-in-poems, was first published in 2007 by Red Hen Press and a new edition was reissued by Sibling Rivalry Press in 2018. Her second book, a biography-in-poems called *Fanny Says*, came out from BOA Editions in 2015 and won the Weatherford Award for Appalachian Poetry. The audio book of that collection came out in 2017. Her poems have, among other places, appeared in *The New York Times*, *The Oxford American*, *Poetry International*, *Gulf Coast*, and *The Best American Poetry 2017*. She has received grants from the National Endowment for the Arts, the Kentucky Foundation for Women, and the Kentucky Arts Council. She was an Assistant Professor at the University of Arkansas at Little Rock for four years until she gave up her beloved time in the classroom in hope of writing full time. Currently, she teaches periodically at a number of places, including the Sewanee School of Letters MFA Program, the Great Smokies Writing Program at UNCA, Poets House, the Poetry Center at Smith College, the Palm Beach Poetry Festival, and the Hindman Settlement School.

She currently lives with her wife, poet Jessica Jacobs, in Asheville, North Carolina, where since 2016 she's volunteered at four different animal sanctuaries. She's at work on a bestiary of sorts about these animals, but she doesn't want it to consist of the kind of pastorals that always made her (and most of the working-class folks she knows) feel shut out of nature and the writing about it—she yearns for poems to speak in a queer, Southern-trash-talking kind of way about nature beautiful, damaged, dangerous, and in desperate need of saving. A chapbook of the first nine poems called *To Those Who Were Our First Gods* won the 2018 Rattle Chapbook Prize. *The Donkey Elegies* is the second result of this project.

ABOUT THE PRESS

SIBLING RIVALRY PRESS is an independent press based in Little Rock, Arkansas. It is a sponsored project of Fractured Atlas, a nonprofit arts service organization. Contributions to support the operations of Sibling Rivalry Press are tax-deductible to the extent permitted by law, and your donations will directly assist in the publication of work that disturbs and enraptures. To contribute to the publication of more books like this one, please visit our website and click *donate*.

Sibling Rivalry Press gratefully acknowledges the following donors, without whom this book would not be possible:

Anonymous (18)
Arkansas Arts Council
John Bateman
W. Stephen Breedlove
Dustin Brookshire
Sarah Browning
Billy Butler
Asher Carter
Don Cellini
Nicole Connolly
Jim Cory
Risa Denenberg
John Gaudin
In Memory of Karen Hayes
Gustavo Hernandez
Amy Holman
Argenta Reading Series
Paige James
Nahal Suzanne Jamir
Allison Joseph
Collin Kelley
Trevor Ketner

Andrea Lawlor
Anthony Lioi
Ed Madden & Bert Easter
Mitchell, Blackstock, Ivers & Sneddon, PLLC
Stephen Mitchell
National Endowment for the Arts
Stacy Pendergrast
Simon Randall
Paul Romero
Randi M. Romo
Carol Rosenfeld
Joseph Ross
In Memory of Bill Rous
Matthew Siegel
Alana Smoot
Katherine Sullivan
Tony Taylor
Leslie Taylor
Hugh Tipping
Guy Traiber
Mark Ward
Robert Wright

CPSIA information can be obtained
at www.ICGtesting.com
Printed in the USA
LVHW101525130122
708276LV00011B/641